Grandad and Me

Chantelle Greenhills

Here I am with my grandad.
We are good friends.

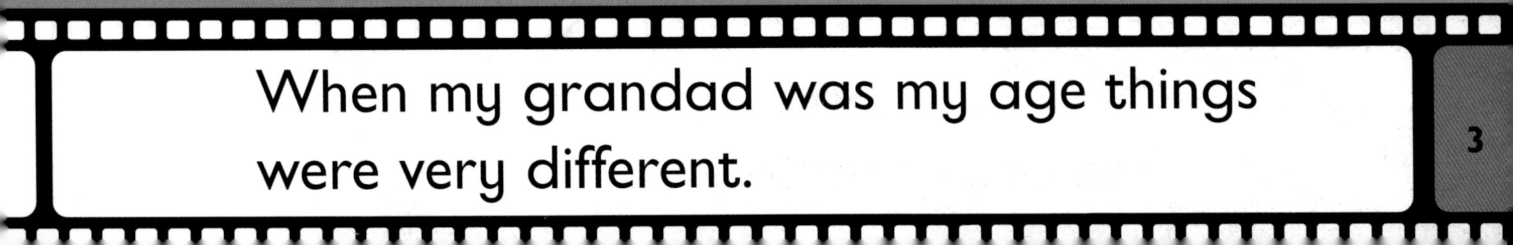

When my grandad was my age things were very different.

Here is my grandad. He is at school.
This is his class photo.

Here I am at school. This is my class photo.

Here is my grandad outside his house.
His house is made of wood.

Here I am. I am outside my house.
My house is made of bricks.

My grandad is eating an ice cream.
It is white ice cream in a wafer.

I am eating an ice cream. My ice cream is brown, orange and green. It is in a cone.

My grandad is playing with a toy. It is a sailing boat and it is his favourite toy.

I am playing with my favourite toy. It is
a computer game.

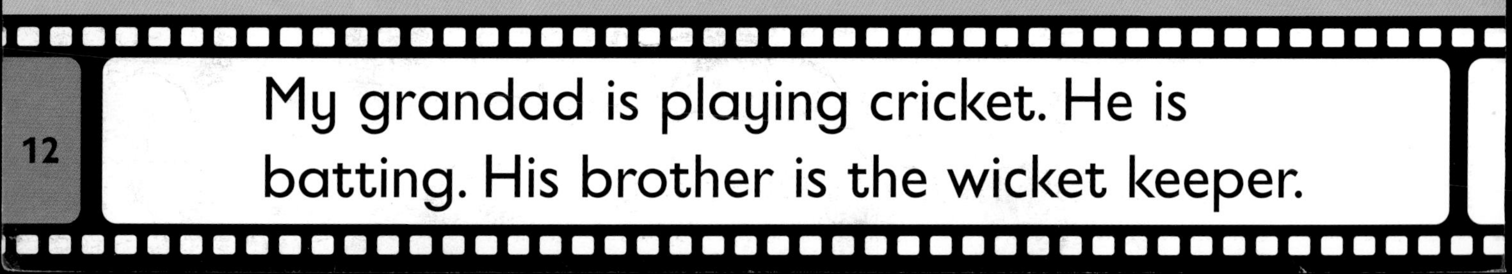

My grandad is playing cricket. He is batting. His brother is the wicket keeper.

I am playing cricket. I am batting
and my mum is bowling.

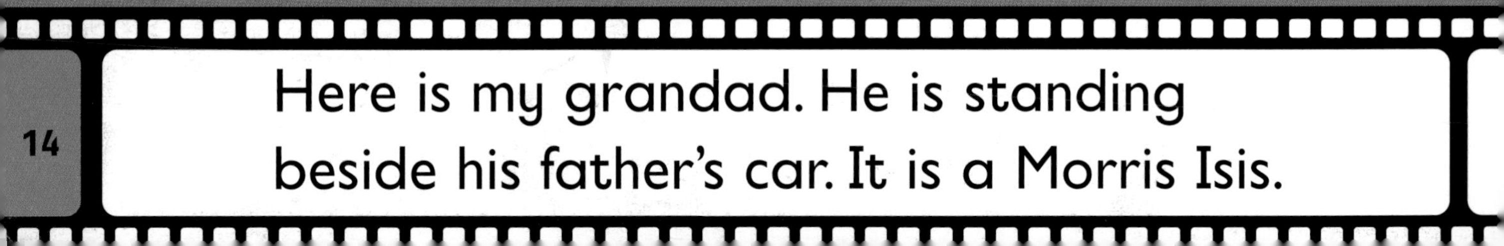

Here is my grandad. He is standing beside his father's car. It is a Morris Isis.

Here I am standing beside my father's car. It is a four-wheel drive car.

Grandad

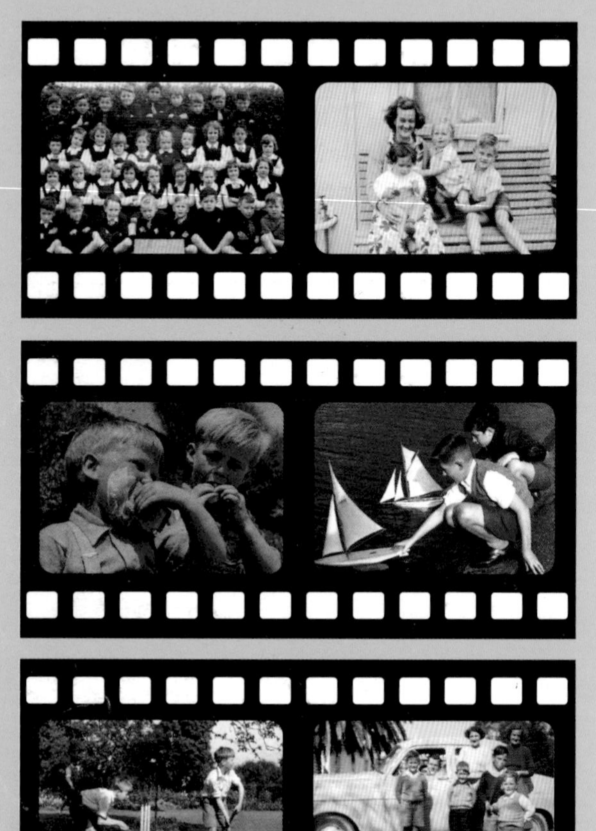

Me